SKILLS FOR REJECTION SENSITIVE DYSPHORIA:

A WORKBOOK FOR TWEENS AND TEENS

Written by Casey O'Brien Martin, LMHC, REAT, RN

Illustrated by Alejandro Ruisánchez

Visit wholechildcounseling.com for additional activities to accompany this book.

DISCLAIMER

Names of people mentioned have been changed to protect the privacy of individuals. The information in this book is not intended or implied to be a substitute for professional medical advice, diagnosis, or treatment. Those responsible for the welfare of children should consult with professionals for matters relating to the child's health and particularly with respect to any symptoms that may require diagnosis or medical attention. If expert assistance or counseling is needed, the services of a competent professional should be sought. Although every effort has been made to ensure that the information in this book is correct at the time of release, the author and publisher do not assume, and hereby disclaim, any liability to any party for any loss, damage, or disruption caused by errors or omissions of details, whether such errors or omissions result from negligence, accident, or any other cause.

SKILLS FOR REJECTION SENSITIVE DYSPHORIA: A WORKBOOK FOR TWEENS AND TEENS

Written by Casey O'Brien Martin, LMHC, REAT, RN

Illustrated by Alejandro Ruisánchez

Published by Whole Child Counseling

Copyright ©2026 Casey O'Brien Martin

ISBN: 978-1-7355177-3-5

TABLE OF CONTENTS

BREATHING TECHNIQUES

TRIGGERS

FEELINGS

COPING SKILLS

SEARCH FOR FACTS

DEAR READER,

I wrote this workbook in a specific order, so the ideas build on each other, but you're in charge of how you use it. You don't have to read this book from start to finish. You can skip around if you want, but before skipping ahead it'll be helpful to read the two comics at the beginning (*Your Brain's Alarm System* and *An Ancient Rejection Alarm*). These comics will help you understand what rejection sensitive dysphoria (RSD) is and why your reactions can feel so big. Once you understand that, you can jump to the sections that feel most useful to you.

This book is about helping you understand what's happening in your brain and body when you experience rejection and giving you some tools to cope.

You don't need to finish every page, write perfect answers, or use every strategy. Some of these skills might feel awkward, difficult, or not very helpful at first, and that's okay. Learning new ways to cope with challenges takes practice, and everyone's brain and body will respond differently. If something doesn't work for you right away, it doesn't mean you're doing it wrong. Just go at your own pace, use what helps now, and come back to the rest later.

YOUR BRAIN'S ALARM SYSTEM

IT CAN FEEL LIKE AN UNBEARABLE PAIN IN YOUR CHEST, LIKE YOU'VE JUST BEEN PUNCHED...
YOUR FACE MIGHT FEEL HOT, YOUR HANDS MIGHT GET SWEATY...
...OR YOUR STOMACH MIGHT GET TWISTED UP LIKE IT'S DOING CARTWHEELS.
...AND YOU MIGHT WANT TO EITHER RUN OR HIDE UNDER YOUR HOODIE AND DISAPPEAR.

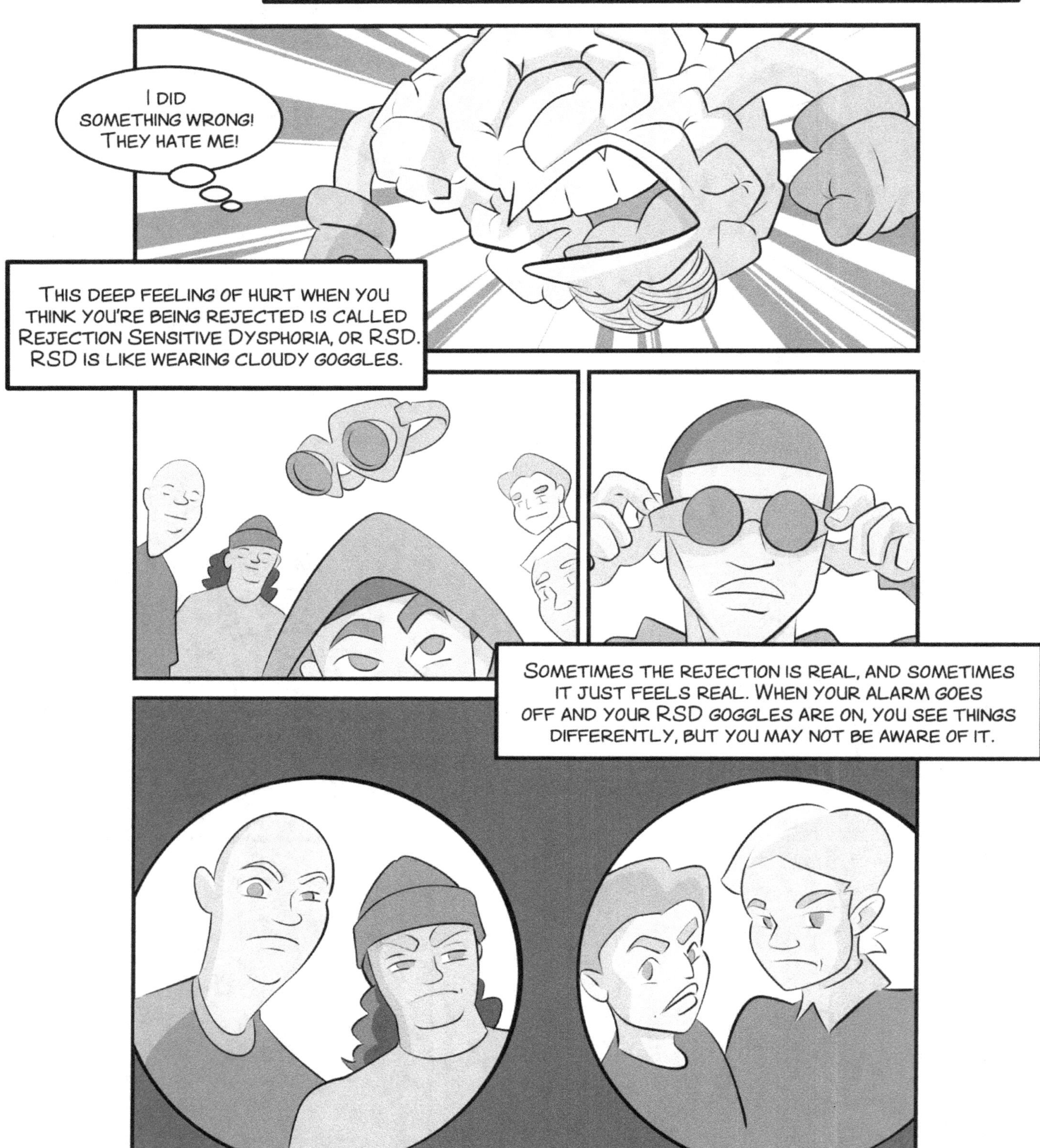

Skills for Rejection Sensitive Dysphoria

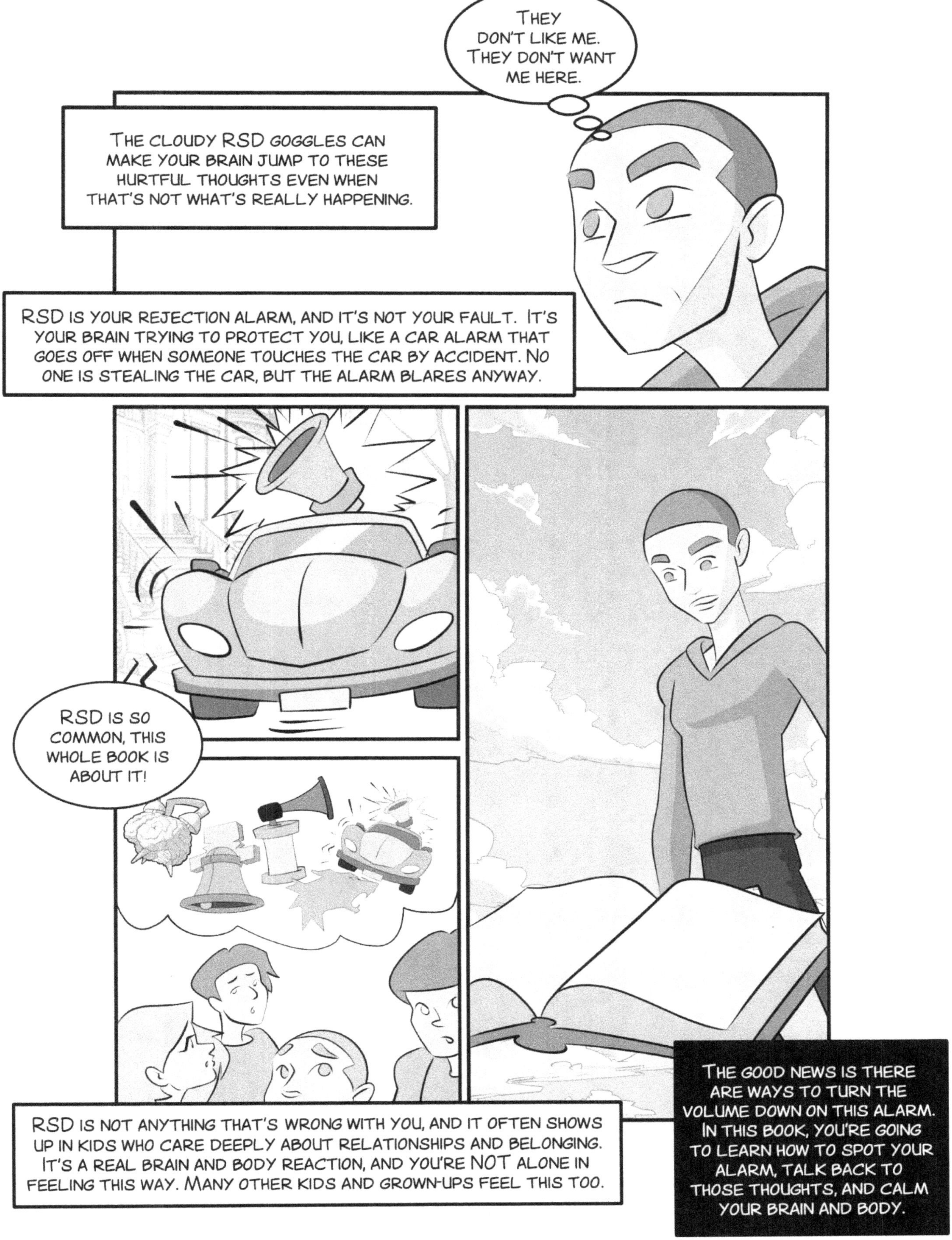

THE CLOUDY RSD GOGGLES CAN MAKE YOUR BRAIN JUMP TO THESE HURTFUL THOUGHTS EVEN WHEN THAT'S NOT WHAT'S REALLY HAPPENING.

RSD IS YOUR REJECTION ALARM, AND IT'S NOT YOUR FAULT. IT'S YOUR BRAIN TRYING TO PROTECT YOU, LIKE A CAR ALARM THAT GOES OFF WHEN SOMEONE TOUCHES THE CAR BY ACCIDENT. NO ONE IS STEALING THE CAR, BUT THE ALARM BLARES ANYWAY.

RSD IS SO COMMON, THIS WHOLE BOOK IS ABOUT IT!

RSD IS NOT ANYTHING THAT'S WRONG WITH YOU, AND IT OFTEN SHOWS UP IN KIDS WHO CARE DEEPLY ABOUT RELATIONSHIPS AND BELONGING. IT'S A REAL BRAIN AND BODY REACTION, AND YOU'RE NOT ALONE IN FEELING THIS WAY. MANY OTHER KIDS AND GROWN-UPS FEEL THIS TOO.

THE GOOD NEWS IS THERE ARE WAYS TO TURN THE VOLUME DOWN ON THIS ALARM. IN THIS BOOK, YOU'RE GOING TO LEARN HOW TO SPOT YOUR ALARM, TALK BACK TO THOSE THOUGHTS, AND CALM YOUR BRAIN AND BODY.

INTRODUCING...

Now that you've learned how your body's alarm works, let's imagine what your inner alarm might look and sound like. In the box below, use lines, colors, shapes, symbols, or words to create your own rejection alarm. Use your creativity and humor! Your alarm might look like a smoke detector, a car horn, a volcano, a bullhorn, a barking dog, or a traffic light. There's no right or wrong way to do this. Just make something that makes sense to you.

NAMING YOUR ALARM

Learning to pause and notice your RSD alarm gives you more power over it. When you give your inner alarm a name, it becomes easier to recognize and talk back to. So now, when you notice your alarm going off and you're having a big emotional reaction, you can picture the alarm you created and think, "Oh, that's just my ancient rejection alarm, _________________, and I know I'm safe right now."

Name Here

MY ALARM'S NAME IS:

____

NOT EVERYTHING YOUR ALARM SAYS IS TRUE!

Put a star next to the hurtful words your alarm has tried to say to you in the past. In the shapes below, write down some of the other hurtful words your alarm tries to shout at you.

AN ANCIENT ALARM IN A MODERN WORLD

OUR BRAINS LEARNED SOMETHING REALLY IMPORTANT: IT WAS SUPER DANGEROUS IF THE GROUP DIDN'T LIKE YOU OR KICKED YOU OUT!
SO, TO KEEP US SAFE, OUR BRAINS CREATED THIS INNER REJECTION ALARM SYSTEM TO WARN US WHEN WE MIGHT BE LEFT OUT OR REJECTED, BECAUSE THAT USED TO MEAN BIG TROUBLE.
FAST FORWARD TO TODAY, AND THERE ISN'T LIFE OR DEATH DANGER FROM BEING KICKED OUT OF THE GROUP. THERE AREN'T SABER-TOOTHED TIGERS TO FACE IF YOU'RE ON YOUR OWN, BUT WE STILL HAVE THAT SAME BRAIN ALARM!

THAT SAME REJECTION ALARM CAN GO OFF DURING EVERYDAY MOMENTS, LIKE A FRIEND NOT ANSWERING YOUR TEXT, SEEING A FRIEND LAUGH WITH SOMEONE ELSE AND ASSUMING IT MEANS YOU DON'T BELONG, OR EVEN WHEN YOUR DOG SNUGGLES UP WITH YOUR BROTHER INSTEAD OF YOU.
do you want to hang out this weekend?
WITH RSD, YOUR ALARM SYSTEM IS EXTRA SENSITIVE, SO IT CAN GO OFF EVEN WHEN THERE ISN'T A REAL REJECTION OR EMERGENCY.
do you want to hang out this weekend?
READ
I KNOW HE HATES ME NOW.
I KNOW I MESSED UP AND DID SOMETHING WRONG.
EVEN MY DOG LIKES HIM BETTER!
THE ALARM IS JUST TRYING TO KEEP YOU SAFE AND HELP YOU BELONG, BUT SOMETIMES IT MISREADS SITUATIONS AND SOUNDS THE ALARM TOO SOON AND TOO LOUDLY.

Your rejection alarm isn't bad or broken. It's just ancient, and when it goes off, it needs helpful reminders that you're actually safe.

Your brain is designed to protect you, so when your brain thinks you're in danger, it sends a message to your body to get ready.

This is called the fight, flight, freeze, or fawn response, and it can even happen when there's no real danger.

Now let's learn about the P.A.U.S.E. strategy, which is a tool to help you when your alarm goes off. Each letter stands for a step:

P AUSE, NOTICE YOUR ALARM, AND BREATHE

A LLOW AND NAME YOUR FEELINGS

U SE A COPING SKILL

S EARCH FOR FACTS

E NCOURAGE YOURSELF

SLOW IT DOWN

Since each letter in the P.A.U.S.E. strategy stands for a step, let's start with the first letter. The letter P stands for: **<u>P</u>ause, Notice Your Alarm, and Breathe.**

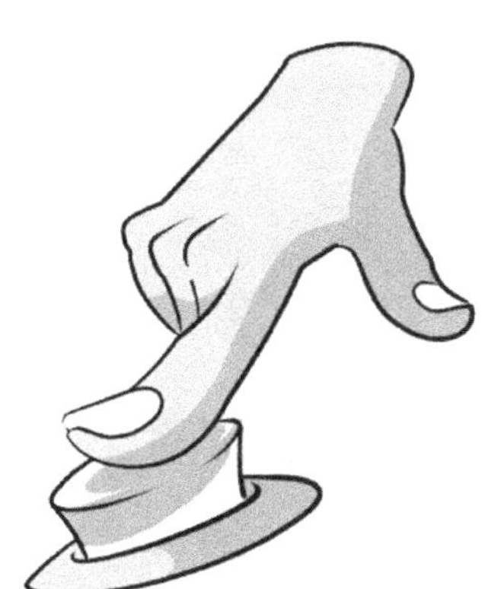

PAUSE

NOTICE YOUR ALARM

BREATHE

When you pause, you interrupt yourself from having a quick reaction. This gives you a chance to slow down. When you notice your alarm, you can understand what's happening in your body. When you take slow, deep breaths, you're sending a signal to your brain that you're safe. Breathing also helps turn off your inner alarm and lets your thinking brain come back online.

WHY IT WORKS

PAUSING GIVES YOU A MOMENT TO STOP. NOTICING YOUR RSD ALARM MAKES YOU MORE AWARE OF WHAT'S GOING ON IN YOUR BODY. BREATHING CHANGES WHAT'S GOING ON BY SLOWING YOUR HEART RATE AND LOWERING THE STRESS CHEMICALS IN YOUR BODY.

BREATHE YOUR WAY TO CALM

It might seem basic, but it really helps to use these breathing techniques when your alarm goes off. Deep breathing helps send a message to your brain that says, "Hey, I'm safe. You can calm down now." When you slow your breathing, it tells your nervous system to turn down the alarm. Breathing helps your heart rate slow down, your muscles unclench, and your thoughts stop racing so you can think more clearly instead of reacting quickly.

Just like learning a game, a sport, or an instrument, breathing strategies work best with practice. Try each of these breathing strategies 3–5 times and rate how each one makes you feel on a 1–10 scale, with 10 being the best.

After that, practice your favorites every day when you're calm and also start using them when your alarm blares loudly. If these feel challenging at first, don't worry. They'll get easier to use with practice.

RESET BREATH

Breathe in twice, quickly through your nose, followed by a long, slow breath out through your mouth. Repeat.

OCEAN BREATH

Breathe in slowly through your nose, then breathe out through your mouth like you're fogging up a mirror, but close your mouth just a little, so you hear a soft ocean wave sound in the back of your throat. Repeat.

FIRST, BREATHE IN
FOR 4 SECONDS

NEXT, HOLD
FOR 1 SECOND

LAST, BREATHE OUT
FOR 6 SECONDS

4-1-6 BREATH

Breathe in for 4 seconds. Hold for 1 second. Breathe out for 6 seconds. Repeat. If you like this, you can also try 4-7-8 breathing.

SUNNY BREATH

Pick a two-syllable word or phrase like "be calm" or "am safe." Breathe in while you think of the first word and breathe out while you think of the second word. For example, breathe in and think "here" and then breathe out and think "now." Repeat.

BOX BREATH

Trace your finger over the box and breathe in for 4. Hold your breath for 4. Breathe out for 4. Hold your breath after breathing out for 4. Repeat.

HIGH-FIVE BREATH

Open your hand up like you're going to give a high-five. Take your other pointer finger and place it at the base of your thumb. Slide it up your thumb slowly as you breathe in and slide it down your thumb slowly as you breathe out. Repeat this movement and breathing for each finger. Then switch and trace the other hand.

FOGHORN BREATH

Take a slow breath in through your nose. As you breathe out, make a low, steady "vooooo" sound, like a foghorn. Feel the gentle vibration in your throat and chest. Repeat.

CREATE A TIERED LIST

Everyone's body responds differently to breathing techniques, so there's no "best" breathing strategy for everyone. The best ones are the ones that work well for you.

Look at the ratings you created for these breathing techniques. Now, create a tiered list by ranking them in order from most helpful to least helpful. Then put a star next to your top 3 and start practicing those 3 every day for a few minutes.

Athletes don't wait until game day to play. They practice every day so their bodies know what to do under pressure during the big game. Your breathing techniques and coping skills work the same way! When you practice them daily while you're calm, they're easier to remember and use when your emotions feel intense.

1. _________________________   5. _________________________

2. _________________________   6. _________________________

3. _________________________   7. _________________________

4. _________________________

NOTICING TRIGGERS

Triggers are situations or thoughts that can set off your rejection alarm, so your brain starts shouting things like "You're not liked!" or "You messed up!" even if these things aren't *actually* true.

Everyone's triggers are different. For one person, a friend not saying hi might hurt a lot, while for someone else, it's getting corrected in front of the class.

If you're aware of your triggers, you can catch your alarm early. This will help you take charge and use your P.A.U.S.E. strategy before you have a big reaction.

RESPOND INSTEAD OF REACT

Your triggers aren't excuses, and just because something triggers your alarm doesn't mean you have to react by blaming yourself, becoming angry, or shutting down. Learning to handle your triggers in a way that helps instead of hurts you gives you more power.

WHY IT WORKS

IT HELPS TO KNOW YOUR TRIGGERS BECAUSE IT ALLOWS YOU TO CATCH YOUR ALARM EARLY, USE YOUR TOOLS, AND RESPOND INSTEAD OF REACT.

WHAT SETS OFF MY ALARM

Read each of these common RSD triggers. Place a checkmark in the box if it's a trigger that sets off your alarm. If you have other triggers not listed, write them on the next page.

- ❑ Feeling left out
- ❑ Seeing friends whisper or laugh nearby
- ❑ A friend not texting, waving, or saying hi back
- ❑ Getting teased, even in a joking way
- ❑ Saying something out loud and no one responds
- ❑ Being interrupted or talked over
- ❑ Getting corrected or asked to redo something
- ❑ Receiving a grade lower than you expected
- ❑ Being called on when you don't know the answer
- ❑ Comparing yourself to others
- ❑ Feeling like no one notices when you try hard
- ❑ Trying really hard and still not doing "good enough"
- ❑ Feeling like someone is mad or disappointed in you
- ❑ Getting a "look" or sigh from someone
- ❑ Being told to hurry up or "you should know this by now"

❑ Getting in trouble

❑ Someone having a tone that sounds annoyed

❑ Making a mistake

❑ Forgetting something or being unprepared

❑ Feeling like you said the wrong thing

❑ Feeling misunderstood or blamed

❑ Not being believed or taken seriously

❑ Thinking that others think you're weird or not good enough

❑ A friend suddenly acting distant or hanging out with someone else

❑ Other triggers: _______________________________________

____

____

____

____

____

____

____

MOMENTS THAT PUSH MY BUTTONS

Life won't always feel fair, and we can't avoid our triggers. Sometimes people will forget to text back, or we might not get picked for every team. The goal isn't to make those moments disappear, it's just to be aware of our triggers so we can know when to use our P.A.U.S.E. strategy.

In the box below, write or draw your biggest triggers, or the situations that set off your alarm.

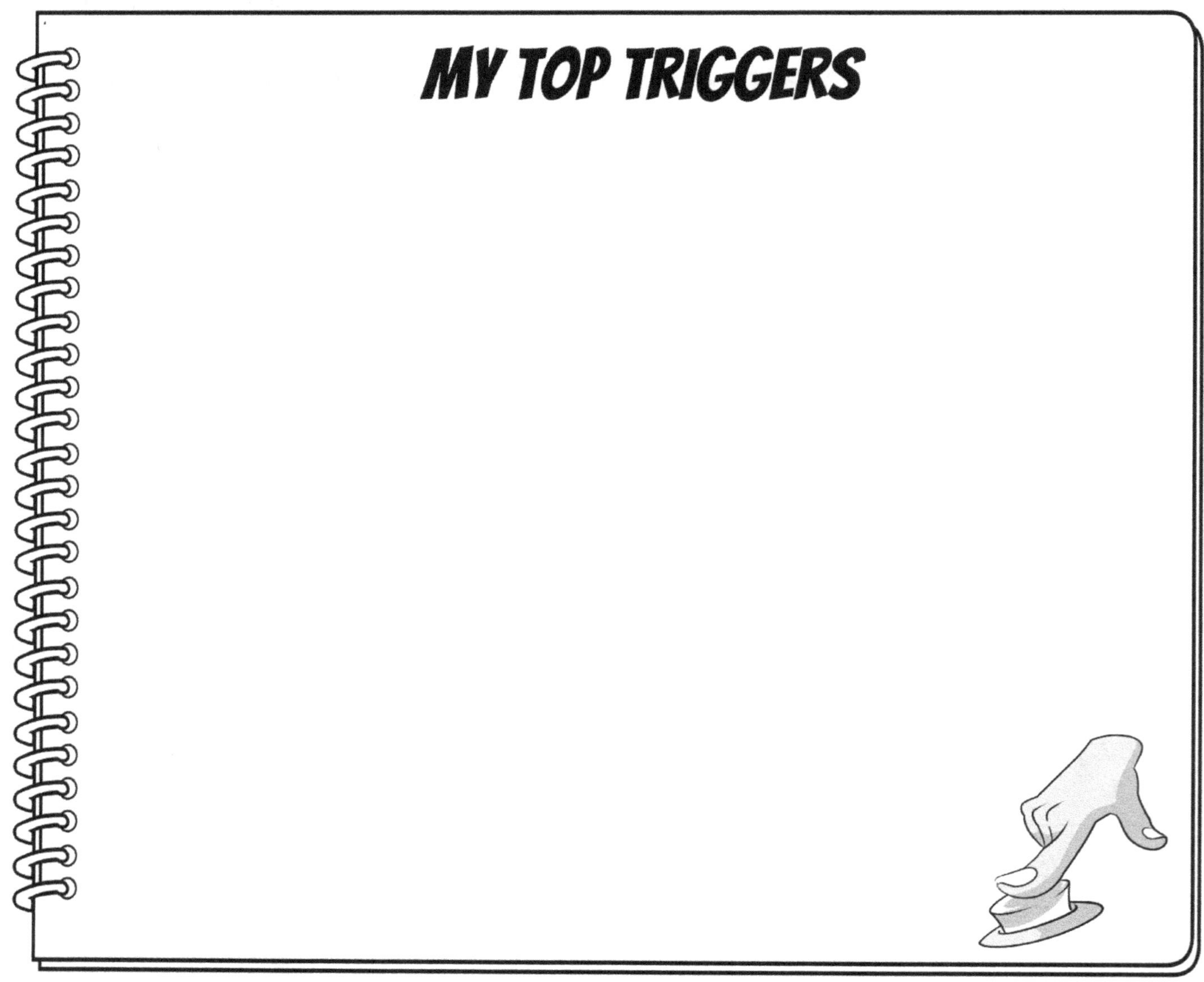

We learned about the strategies for the letter P. Now let's look at the strategy that goes along with the letter A.

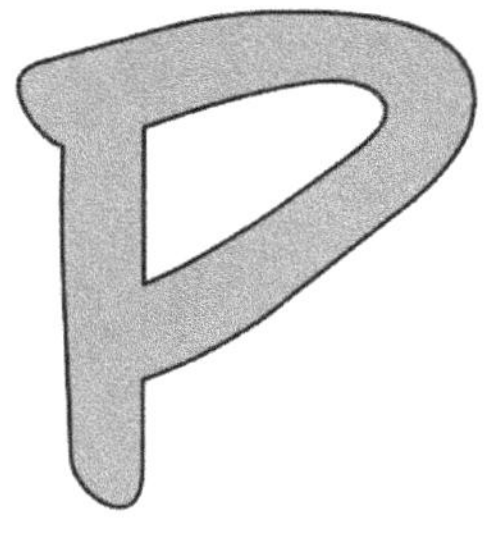 **P**AUSE, NOTICE YOUR ALARM, AND BREATHE 

 **A**LLOW AND NAME YOUR FEELINGS 

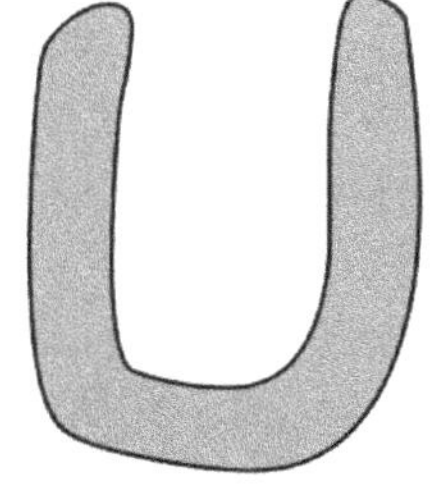 **U**SE A COPING SKILL 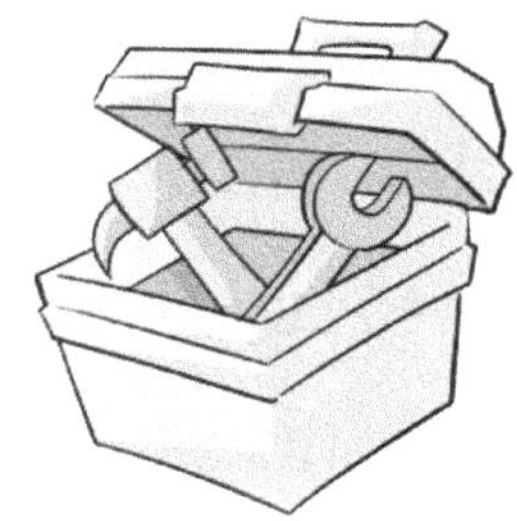

 **S**EARCH FOR FACTS 

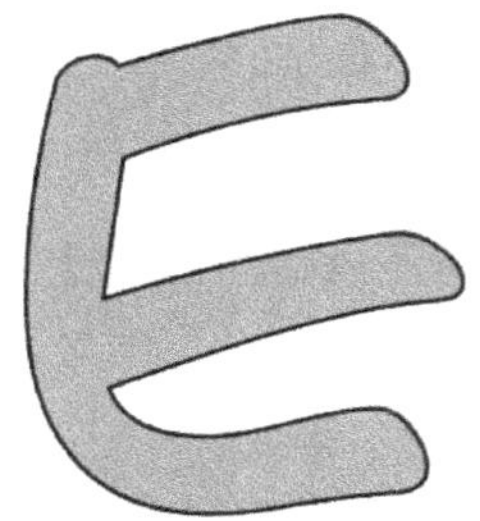 **E**NCOURAGE YOURSELF 

ALLOW AND NAME YOUR FEELINGS

The letter A in P.A.U.S.E. stands for: **Allow and Name Your Feelings.**

Experiencing feelings is part of being human, and you should never feel ashamed or embarrassed about your feelings. You'll experience and move through your emotions more quickly if you notice them and allow them to flow through you without resisting them. In fact, when you try to resist or stuff your feelings down, they often come back bigger and stronger!

Scientists have found that when we experience an emotion, the chemicals in our brains and bodies last for about 90 seconds. This is the total amount of time from when the trigger happens to when those stress chemicals stop being released. So, if we still have strong feelings after 90 seconds, it's because we keep thinking about what triggered us. Naming your feelings helps your brain make sense of what's happening inside you. When you put words to a feeling, like "I feel ashamed," your thinking brain can turn back on and your alarm starts to quiet down. Noticing, naming, and allowing your feelings makes them easier to move through. Even the biggest feelings will pass, especially

WHY IT WORKS

PUSHING FEELINGS DOWN CAN MAKE THEM POP BACK UP LATER. LETTING FEELINGS MOVE THROUGH YOUR BODY HELPS YOU FEEL CALMER AND MORE IN CONTROL.

when you don't resist them and you let them roll through your body.

Feelings are like tunnels with a beginning, a middle, and an end. You can imagine that you are the car that enters the beginning of the feelings tunnel, goes through the middle of it, and then comes out the other side. When you notice, name, and allow your feelings, you will move through the tunnel even faster.

AFTER HE PAUSES, NOTICES HIS ALARM, AND BREATHES, HE ALLOWS AND NAMES HIS FEELINGS.
IT'S WRONG TO FEEL THIS WAY.
THERE'S MY ALARM. I FEEL EMBARRASSED.
WHEN YOU STUFF FEELINGS DOWN, THEY COME BACK BIGGER.
ANXIETY
EMBARRASSED
SHAME
DESPAIR
WHEN YOU NAME AND ALLOW YOUR FEELINGS, THEY MOVE THROUGH MORE QUICKLY.

LISTENING TO YOUR BODY

Everyone's body gives different signals when their alarm goes off. Some people might feel it in their chest, stomach, or face. Other people might notice their muscles tighten, or they might feel like they want to freeze, run, or hide. There's no right way. It's just each person's body letting them know something feels off.

Think of times when your alarm went off and you were feeling rejected, embarrassed, left out, criticized, or like someone didn't like you. Then place a checkmark next to the words below that match how your body felt in those moments. If there are other words that describe the sensations in your body during those moments, write them on the lines below.

WHY IT WORKS

MAPPING YOUR BODY HELPS YOU NOTICE YOUR CUES, RECOGNIZE YOUR ALARM EARLY, AND STAY MORE IN CONTROL.

☐ TIGHT	☐ SWIRLY	☐ ACHY
☐ HEAVY	☐ WOBBLY	☐ _______________
☐ HOT	☐ STIFF	☐ _______________
☐ JUMPY	☐ FROZEN	☐ _______________
☐ SHAKY	☐ BUZZING	☐ _______________
☐ TINGLY	☐ SQUEEZED	☐ _______________

MAPPING THE ALARM

In the body outline below, map out where you feel rejection in your body. Use colors, lines, shapes, words, or symbols to show what happens in your body when your alarm goes off. Be creative and have fun! There's no right way to do this.

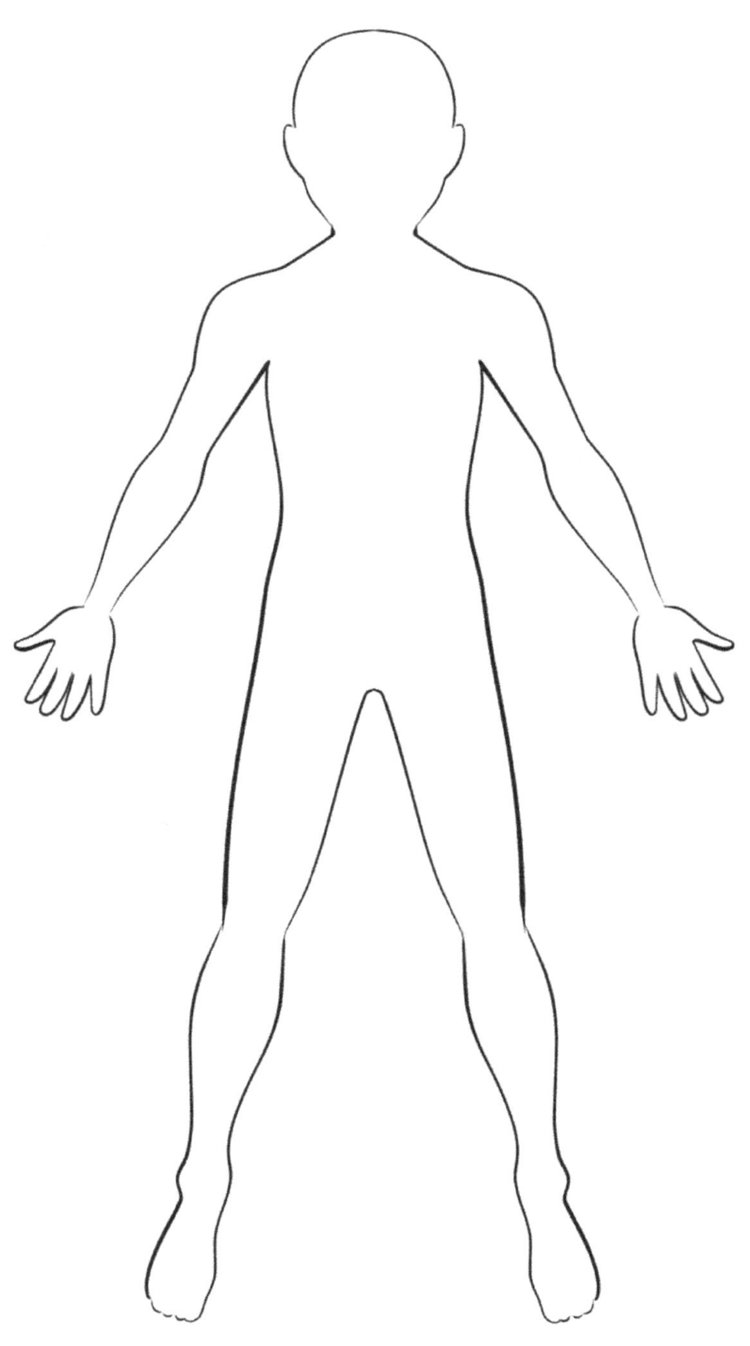

We learned about the steps for the letters P and A. Now let's look at the strategy that goes along with the letter U.

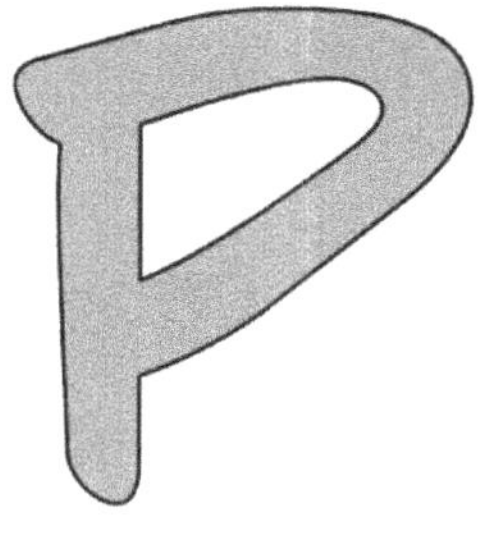 **P**AUSE, NOTICE YOUR ALARM, AND BREATHE 

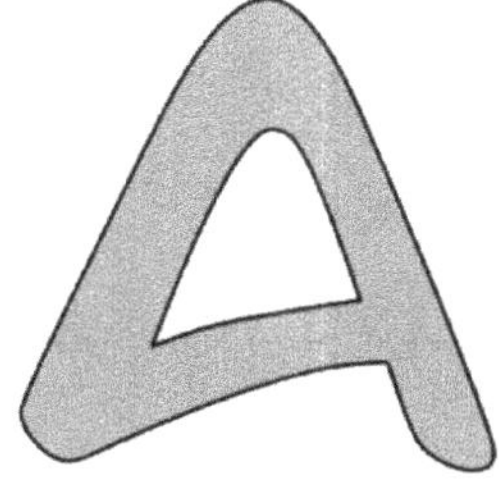 **A**LLOW AND NAME YOUR FEELINGS 

 **U**SE A COPING SKILL 

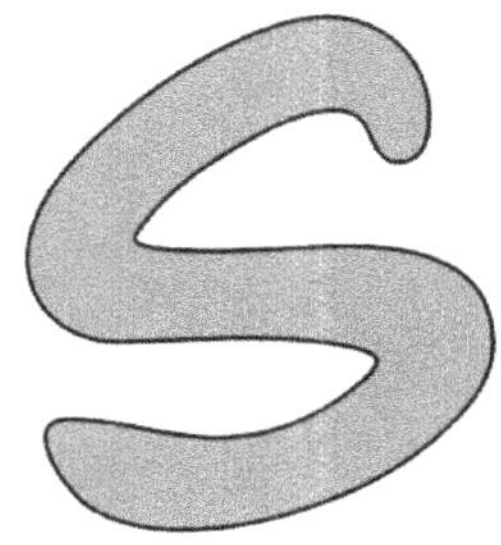 **S**EARCH FOR FACTS 

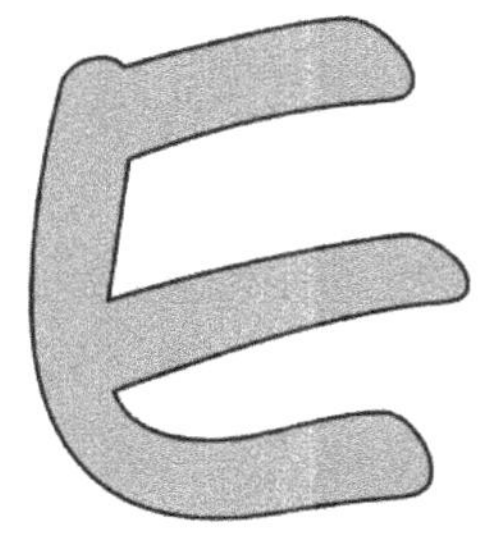 **E**NCOURAGE YOURSELF 

USING COPING SKILLS

The letter U in the P.A.U.S.E. strategy stands for <u>**Use a Coping Skill.**</u>

When your rejection alarm is loud, your body might feel tight, hot, shaky, or restless. Before you can think clearly again, coping skills help to calm your body down.

Coping skills are like tools in your toolbox. Not every tool works for every job, so try them out to find the ones that work best for you. You might even find that it's helpful to use a few coping skills together at one time.

USING COLD TO CALM

When intense feelings hit, your body needs a strong signal to slow down, and feeling something cold can help with that. Using something cold wakes up your senses and tells your brain, "Pause. I'm here. I'm safe."

Cold works especially well when your alarm feels loud, your thoughts are racing, or your body feels shaky or overwhelmed. You're not trying to get rid of your feelings, you're just helping your body calm down enough so you can control your thoughts. Cold should feel refreshing and not painful, so choose what feels safe and comfortable for you.

Try it out:

- ❑ Take a cool shower
- ❑ Step outside into cool air
- ❑ Drink a few sips of cold water
- ❑ Splash cold water on your face or wrists
- ❑ Hold an ice cube, a cold soda can, or a metal water bottle
- ❑ Press a cold washcloth on your face or on the back of your neck
- ❑ Place a spoon in the fridge or freezer, then hold it on your palm or face

WHY IT WORKS

COLD HELPS CALM YOUR BODY BY GIVING YOUR BRAIN A STRONG RESET SIGNAL. IT TURNS DOWN THE ALARM AND HELPS YOU FEEL MORE GROUNDED.

SOUR RESET

You can taste something sour to quickly wake up your senses and break out of an emotional spiral. You might suck on a sour candy or taste something sour like a gummy, a lemon, or a lime.

The sharp sour taste gives your brain something very clear to focus on. Remember, the sour taste should feel intense but not painful.

Try it out: Taste something sour and notice how it pulls your attention right to the present moment.

WHY IT WORKS

SOUR FOOD WORKS BECAUSE THE STRONG TASTE GRABS YOUR BRAIN'S ATTENTION RIGHT AWAY. THAT SHARP SENSATION PULLS YOU OUT OF RACING THOUGHTS, BRINGS YOU BACK INTO THE PRESENT MOMENT, AND HELPS YOUR NERVOUS SYSTEM RESET SO YOUR ALARM CAN CALM DOWN.

HAPPY MEMORIES

A happy memory is like a favorite moment you can replay in your mind to help your body relax. It could be a time you laughed really hard, felt proud of yourself, had fun with friends, or felt loved and supported. When you remember a positive moment in detail your brain and body can start to feel some of those same calm, happy feelings again. This helps shift your brain out of alarm mode and reminds you that good things have happened and will happen again.

Try it out: Close your eyes and replay one happy memory like watching a short movie for 10–20 seconds. Notice one thing you saw, heard, felt, and did in that moment.

WHY IT WORKS

WHEN YOU REMEMBER A HAPPY MOMENT IN DETAIL, YOUR BRAIN SENDS CALMING SIGNALS TO YOUR BODY, ALMOST LIKE YOU'RE THERE AGAIN. THIS HELPS TURN DOWN YOUR ALARM AND REMINDS YOU THAT YOU'RE SAFE AND THAT GOOD MOMENTS ARE REAL AND POSSIBLE.

SIDE GAZE

Side gaze is a gentle movement with your neck and eyes that helps your body switch into a calm, relaxed state.

Try it out: Sit in your chair and gently lower your head to the right side, so your right ear is lowered toward your right shoulder. Then, without moving your head, slide your eyes all the way to the right and gently look off to the side. Stay there for about 30 seconds. Your mouth might water, or you might have the urge to yawn or swallow. These are signs that your body is relaxing.

Now, bring your head back to center.

Then, gently lower your head to the left side, so your left ear is lowered toward your left shoulder. Then, without moving your head, slide your eyes all the way to the left and gently look off to the side. Stay there for about 30 seconds.

You might notice some of those same signs that your body is relaxing.

Now, bring your head back to center.

WHY IT WORKS

TILTING YOUR HEAD AND MOVING YOUR EYES TO THE SIDE ACTIVATES THE VAGUS NERVE, WHICH SENDS A CALMING SIGNAL THROUGH YOUR NERVOUS SYSTEM AND HELPS YOUR BODY RELAX.

BRAIN DISTRACTIONS

Sometimes our emotions feel so overwhelming that they take over everything. We might feel like our brain is stuck on one upsetting, unhelpful thought, like it's playing on a loop that won't stop. These are the times when a brain distraction can help break the loop.

Distraction doesn't mean ignoring your feelings forever. It just means giving your brain a quick job to do while your emotions calm down. When you have strong feelings, it can be like your computer overheating. Distraction turns the fan on so it can cool down enough for you to think clearly again. You're not trying to "fix" your feelings, you're just helping your brain get unstuck.

WHY IT WORKS

BRAIN DISTRACTIONS WORK BECAUSE THEY GIVE YOUR MIND SOMETHING SIMPLE AND NEUTRAL TO FOCUS ON. THIS HELPS INTERRUPT THE LOOP OF UNHELPFUL THOUGHTS AND GIVES YOUR NERVOUS SYSTEM TIME TO CALM DOWN. ONCE YOUR BRAIN COOLS OFF, IT'S EASIER TO THINK MORE CLEARLY AND FOLLOW THE P.A.U.S.E. STRATEGY.

BRAIN DISTRACTIONS TO TRY

- ❑ Say the alphabet backward

- ❑ Watch a funny or satisfying video

- ❑ Count backward from 100 by 7s or 3s

- ❑ Create a fake menu for a new restaurant

- ❑ Pick a topic and list all you know about it

- ❑ Spell your name and other words backward

- ❑ Name one animal for each letter of the alphabet

- ❑ Count all the square-shaped or blue objects you can find in the room

- ❑ Pick a letter of the alphabet and name words that start with that letter

- ❑ Make a "Top 10" list of favorite songs, games, snacks, places to go, movies, or animals

- ❑ Solve a brain teaser like a riddle, maze, sudoku, word search, or crossword puzzle

- ❑ Describe how something tastes, smells, feels, sounds, and looks in your imagination

❑ Create a secret code by switching each letter with a number or symbol, and write a message to someone

❑ Pick a color and name as many objects as you can think of that are that color

❑ Name as many animals, foods, songs, sports teams, books, tools, states, cities, bodies of water, singers, video games, streamers, or movies as you can think of

Use the box below to list or draw more brain distraction ideas you can try. Think about ways to connect them to things you already enjoy.

MORE BRAIN DISTRACTIONS TO TRY

TAPPING ON YOUR CHEST

Chest tapping is a simple, rhythmic way to calm your body. You can lightly tap or pat the center of your chest with your fingers or hand, almost like a gentle drum, while you breathe slowly.

The steady rhythm and tapping sensation gives your brain something predictable to focus on instead of your strong feelings. This can help turn down your alarm, slow your thoughts, and make your body feel more settled from the inside out.

Try it out: Place one hand or two fingers in the center of your chest. Tap or pat gently in a slow, steady rhythm, like a soft drumbeat. As you tap, take slow breaths in through your nose and out through your mouth. Keep tapping for about one minute and notice if your breathing slows or your body starts to feel calm or steady.

WHY IT WORKS

CHEST TAPPING WORKS BECAUSE THE RHYTHM HELPS CALM YOUR NERVOUS SYSTEM AND QUIETS YOUR ALARM.

CALMING YOUR MIND WITH SOUND

Your voice is one of the fastest ways to send your brain a message that you're safe. Humming, singing, gargling, and even yawning all create gentle vibrations in your throat and chest that help turn down your body's alarm system and bring your nervous system back to calm. These tools are especially helpful when your thoughts feel stuck or you're experiencing intense emotions.

You don't need to sound "good" or do this loudly. You just need to use your voice in a way that feels good for you. Different sounds work for different people, so try a few and notice which ones help your body feel calmer.

WHY IT WORKS

SOUNDS AND VIBRATIONS ACTIVATE THE VAGUS NERVE IN YOUR BODY, WHICH HELPS CALM YOUR NERVOUS SYSTEM. THAT'S WHY USING YOUR VOICE CAN BE JUST AS POWERFUL AS BREATHING.

SOUND STRATEGIES TO TRY

Singing: Sing one of your favorite songs.

Humming: Take a slow breath in and hum as you breathe out slowly, making a gentle "mmmm" sound. Focus on the vibration in your chest and throat. You can even try humming a song.

Gargling: Take a small sip of water and tilt your head back slightly. Open your mouth and gargle by gently making a bubbling sound in your throat while the water moves around. Continue gargling for a few seconds and focus on the vibration in your throat. Then spit the water out.

Yawning: Let yourself yawn or gently fake a yawn 3-4 times if one doesn't come naturally.

In the box below, write down a list of songs that you could try to sing or hum.

FAVORITE SONGS

MOVEMENT

When strong feelings show up, your body has extra energy that needs somewhere to go. Moving your body helps release that energy and tells your brain it's safe to slow down. You don't have to do a full body workout, just a few moments of movement can help your body settle and reset.

WHY IT WORKS

MOVEMENT HELPS YOUR BODY RELEASE STRESS ENERGY TO CLOSE THE STRESS CYCLE. IT ALSO HELPS RESET YOUR NERVOUS SYSTEM.

Here are some movement ideas you can try:

- ❑ Playing a sport
- ❑ Shoulder rolls
- ❑ Wall push-ups
- ❑ Jumping jacks
- ❑ Dancing to music
- ❑ Cat-cow stretch
- ❑ Slow arm circles
- ❑ Rocking side to side
- ❑ Taking a short walk

- ❑ Balancing on one foot

- ❑ Running or marching in place

- ❑ Seated twists in a chair

- ❑ Hugging your knees and rocking

- ❑ Pushing against a wall or table

- ❑ Shaking out your arms and legs

- ❑ Pressing your feet firmly into the floor

- ❑ Stretching your neck gently side to side

- ❑ Doing a slow forward fold and hanging your arms

- ❑ Lying on your back and bringing your knees to your chest

MORE MOVEMENT ACTIVITIES TO TRY

CREATIVE EXPRESSION

Creative expression is a way to let your feelings come out without having to explain them with words. Sometimes it's hard to talk about intense feelings, and creating gives them somewhere safe to go. You can draw, color, write, paint, build, sculpt, or create in any way that feels good for you. There's no right or wrong way to do it! You don't have to make something "pretty" or show it to anyone.

WHY IT WORKS

CREATING HELPS BECAUSE YOU'RE MOVING FEELINGS OUT OF YOUR BODY AND MIND AND INTO SOMETHING YOU CAN SEE AND TOUCH. THIS CAN MAKE EMOTIONS FEEL LESS INTENSE, HELP YOUR BODY CALM DOWN, AND MAKE IT EASIER TO UNDERSTAND WHAT YOU'RE FEELING.

CREATIVE IDEAS TO EXPLORE

- ☐ Build an island

- ☐ Create your family as animals

- ☐ Turn a problem into a doodle maze

- ☐ Make a map of your day as a journey

- ☐ Draw or doodle with your eyes closed

- ☐ Create a superhero version of yourself

- ☐ Draw your thoughts as speech bubbles

- ☐ Write a poem or song about a safe place

- ☐ Turn your feelings into a monster and draw it

- ☐ Draw with the hand you don't usually draw with

- ☐ Draw what your worry looks like if it had a shape

- ☐ Draw about your week using only lines and shapes

- ☐ Make a collage about your past, present, and future

- ☐ Draw yourself before, during, and after strong feelings

- ☐ Write a poem or song where each line starts with "I am"

- ☐ Make a comic about something that happened this year

- ☐ Draw something in the room, but never lift your pencil from the paper

CREATIVE BRAINSTORM

In the box below, draw, write, doodle, or brainstorm a list of creative ideas you might want to explore in the future.

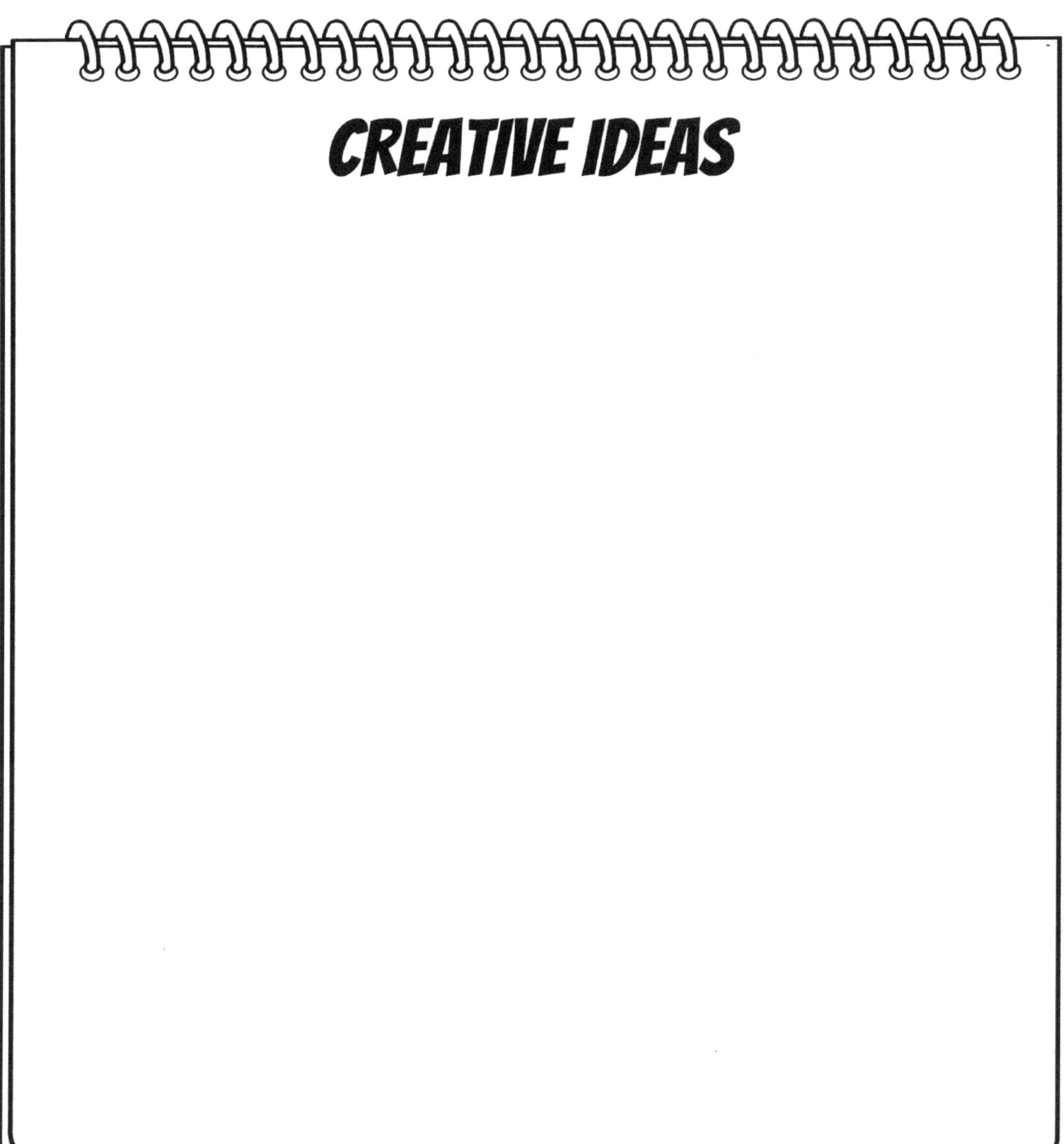

AFFECTION

Affection is using safe, comforting touch to help your body feel secure. This could be a 20-second hug with someone you trust, holding someone's hand, or snuggling with a pet. When you feel connected to someone who cares about you, your body gets the message, "I'm not alone."

Hugs, cuddles, and gentle touch can slow your heart rate, relax your muscles, and release calming chemicals in your brain. Even snuggling with or petting a dog or cat can help your nervous system settle and make your feelings easier to handle.

Try it out: Cuddle with a pet or ask a trusted person for a hug.

WHY IT WORKS

AFFECTION WORKS BECAUSE SAFE TOUCH HELPS YOUR BODY FEEL SUPPORTED AND CALM, WHICH TURNS DOWN YOUR INNER ALARM.

SELF-MASSAGE

Self-massage means using your hands to gently press or rub your muscles to help your body relax and feel calmer. You might massage your ears, your hands, your shoulders, or your neck.

Massage helps relax tight muscles and reminds your body that it's okay to soften. The pressure and warmth of your hands send calming signals through your nervous system to help you feel more grounded.

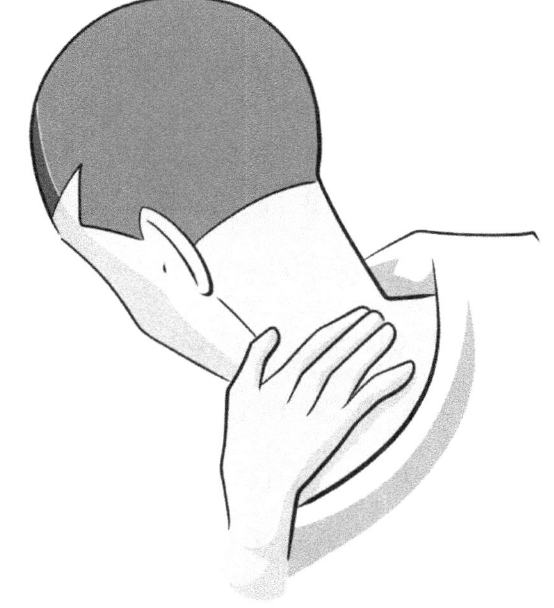

Try it out: Rub your hands together to warm them up. If it feels comfortable, gently squeeze and massage one hand at a time, starting at your fingers and moving toward your wrist. Use your fingertips to gently rub your shoulders or the sides of your neck. If it feels right, softly massage the outside of your ears using small circles. Take a slow breath in and out as you massage and notice if your body starts to feel a little softer or calmer.

WHY IT WORKS

SELF-MASSAGE WORKS BECAUSE GENTLE TOUCH HELPS YOUR MUSCLES RELAX AND TELLS YOUR BODY IT'S OKAY TO CALM DOWN.

GROUNDING

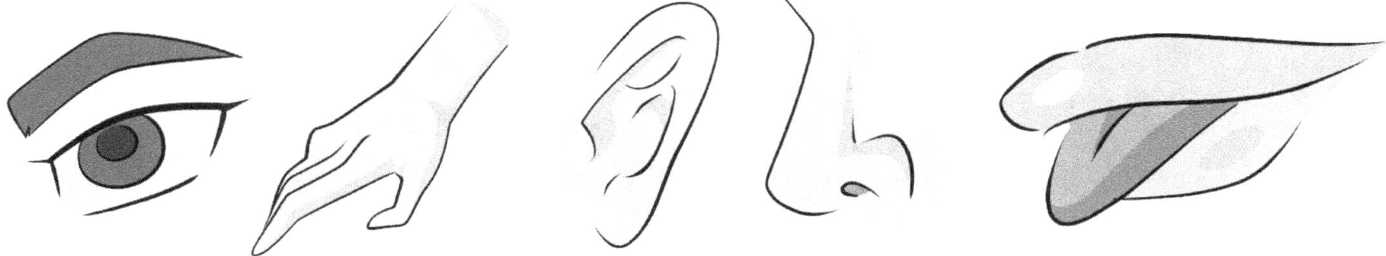

Grounding is a helpful skill to use if you feel anxious or overwhelmed because it helps you become aware of the present moment that's happening right now. When your brain gets stuck in intense emotions like fear, embarrassment, or panic, it can start to feel like everything is spinning or unsafe, even if nothing dangerous is *actually* happening. These are moments when your brain needs help remembering, "I'm right here. I'm okay. I'm safe."

When you look around and name what you can see, hear, feel, smell, and taste, your brain realizes, "Oh, I know where I am. I don't have to panic."

Try it out: Look around you. Take a slow, deep breath. Use your senses to name 5 things you can see. Name 4 things you can touch. Name 3 things you can hear. Name 2 things you can smell, and name 1 thing you can taste.

WHY IT WORKS

GROUNDING USES YOUR FIVE SENSES TO BRING YOUR BRAIN BACK TO THE PRESENT MOMENT. GROUNDING CAN HELP YOU TURN OFF THE ALARM BY INTERRUPTING RACING THOUGHTS AND GETTING YOU OUT OF YOUR HEAD AND INTO YOUR BODY.

CREATE A GROUNDING SENSORY BOX

Find a box and fill it with items that help calm you. Include a few soothing items for each of your senses. For sight, you might add a calming picture or a positive message. For touch, you might try slime, a stress ball, satisfying fabric, or a smooth stone. For hearing, you could include a chime or headphones for music. For smell, you could add rosewater, or a favorite calming scent, like lavender on a cotton ball. For taste, you might include gum, a mint, or a sour candy.

When your alarm goes off, you can pause, notice it, take a slow breath, and then open your sensory box and choose one or two items to focus on for a few minutes.

VISUALIZATION

Visualization means using your imagination to picture something. You might imagine a peaceful place like a beach, a forest, a cozy room, a bubble of protection around you, or a future moment where things go well.

Try it out:

If you're comfortable, close your eyes or soften your gaze. Take a slow breath in and out. Picture a place where you feel calm and safe. It could be a real or imaginary place. Picture what you would see, hear, smell, and feel if you were there. Stay with that image for a few breaths and let your body settle into the calm feeling it brings. Your body can start to relax and your feelings can soften.

WHY IT WORKS

WHEN YOU IMAGINE SOMETHING CALM OR SAFE, YOUR BRAIN RESPONDS LIKE IT'S REAL. THIS HELPS YOUR BODY RELAX, SLOWS YOUR BREATHING, AND TURNS DOWN YOUR INNER ALARM.

In the box below, write or draw some of the peaceful places you can practice visualizing. They can be real, imaginary, or a combination of the two.

PEACEFUL PLACES

SQUEEZE AND RELAX YOUR MUSCLES

When your body holds on to feelings like stress or fear without you even noticing, you can help your nervous system feel calmer by gently squeezing then relaxing different parts of your body. This helps your brain and body work together as a team.

Try it out: First, wiggle around in your chair until you find a spot where you feel cozy. If it feels comfortable to you, pretend you're squeezing a watermelon between your arms and bring your arms in close to your body to make your muscles tight. Hold for 3... 2... 1... Now, slowly let go and let your arms drop gently down. Notice if your arms feel heavier or softer.

Now, when you're ready, push your legs down into the chair like you're trying to stay grounded during a storm. Squeeze your leg muscles, just a little, not too hard. Hold for 3... 2... 1... Now release and let your legs feel heavy and relaxed.

Next, if you'd like to, you can pretend you're grabbing sand with your toes. Curl them up tightly. Squeeze and hold for 3... 2... 1... Now slowly uncurl and stretch your toes.

If it feels comfortable, you can gently tighten your belly like you're bracing for a cold splash of water. Hold the tension in your core, just enough to notice and hold for 3... 2... 1... Then let go. Let your belly soften and feel your breath move more easily.

Now, if it feels right for you in this moment, sit up tall and try to gently press your back into the chair. Tighten your back muscles like you're holding a superhero pose. Hold for 3... 2... 1... Then relax back into the chair and let your spine feel supported.

If it feels right for you, take a slow, deep breath in through your nose... Hold it... And then let it out slowly through your mouth like you're blowing out a candle.

WHY IT WORKS

TENSING A MUSCLE HELPS YOUR BRAIN NOTICE IT. LETTING IT GO HELPS YOUR BRAIN FEEL THE RELIEF, AND THAT RELEASE IS HOW YOUR BODY LEARNS TO LET GO.

FINDING WHAT WORKS

Not every coping skill will work for you, and that's okay. They're tools, and different ones will work better for different people. You might even find it's helpful to combine multiple skills and use them together. Each time you try a new skill, rate it on a scale from 1–10, with 10 being the best. Write each number below.

Using Cold to Calm: ____

Sour Reset: ____

Happy Memories: ____

Side Gaze: ____

Brain Distractions: ____

Tapping on Your Chest: ____

Sound Strategies: ____

Movement: ____

Creative Expression: ____

Affection: ____

Self-Massage: ____

Grounding: ____

Visualization: ____

Squeeze and Relax Your Muscles: ____

In the box below, write or draw any other coping skills that work well for you. These might be things you already do, ideas from your life, or other strategies you want to try.

Look over your ratings on the previous page and create a tiered list. Write the top five coping skills that you find most helpful and rank them. These will be your go-to tools to practice and use.

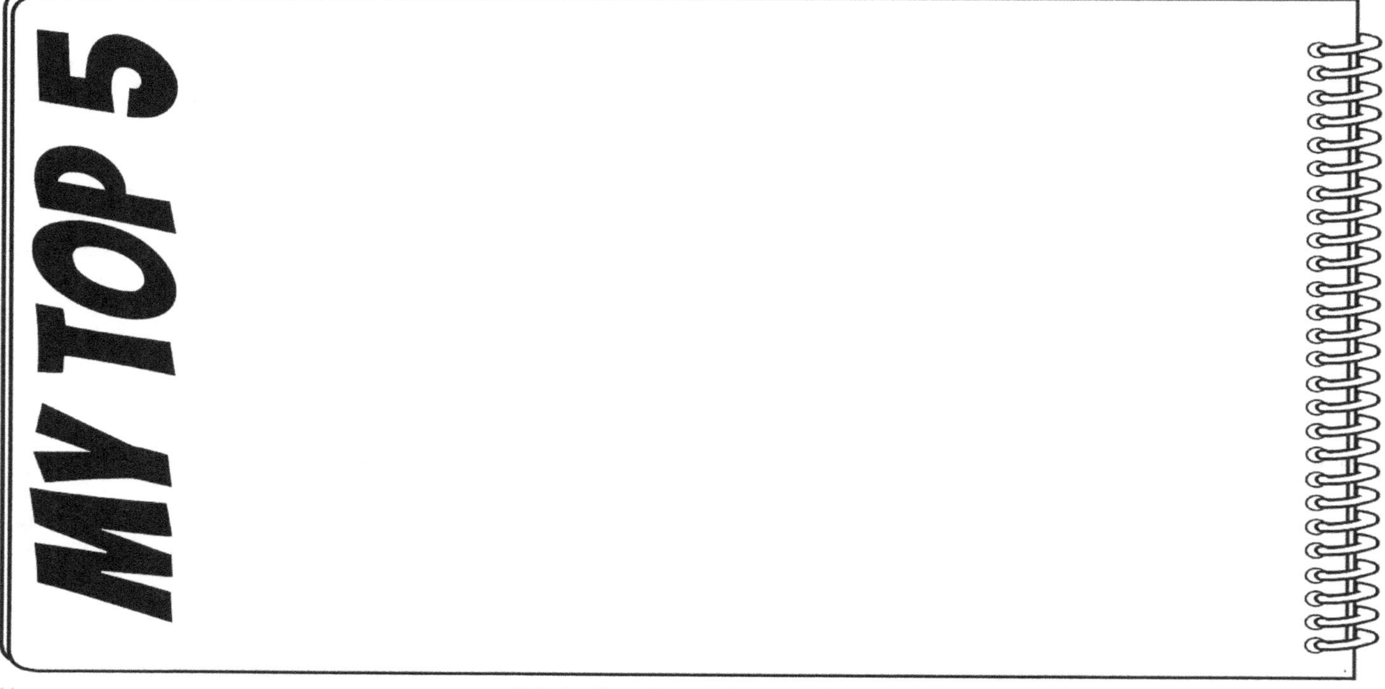

We learned about the steps for the letters P, A, and U. Now let's look at the strategy that goes along with the letter S.

P AUSE, NOTICE YOUR ALARM, AND BREATHE

A LLOW AND NAME YOUR FEELINGS

U SE A COPING SKILL

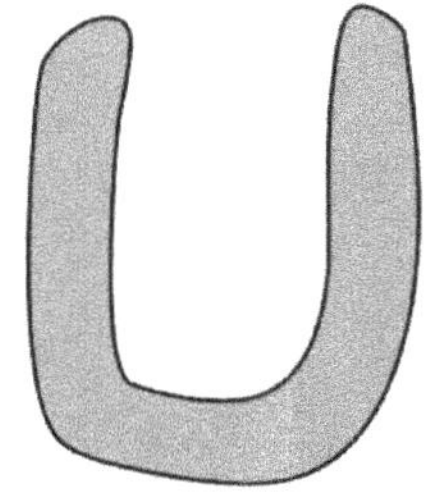 

S EARCH FOR FACTS

E NCOURAGE YOURSELF

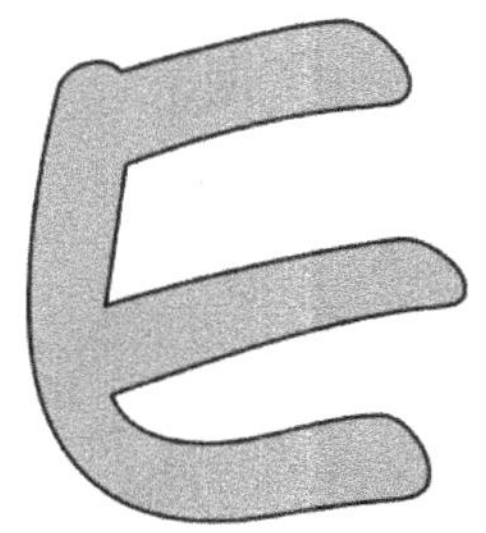 

SEARCH FOR FACTS

The S in P.A.U.S.E. stands for **<u>S</u>earch for Facts**. When your RSD alarm goes off, your thoughts can start sounding very convincing. You might even start believing things like "They don't like me" or "I messed everything up," even if there's no real proof! That's because when you have your RSD goggles on, your brain can misread what's happening.

Here is something important: A thought is not the same thing as a fact, and **not everything you think is true**. Your feelings are real, but your thoughts don't always tell the full story.

When you search for facts, you're checking whether the story your alarm is telling you is the only possible explanation, or whether there might be other explanations too. You're acting like a detective, looking for clues instead of jumping to conclusions. When you're searching for facts, you can get curious by asking yourself these questions:

- *What's the story my brain is telling me right now?*

- *What proof do I have that this story is true?*

- *What proof do I have that it might not be true?*

- *Is there another way to look at this situation?*

- *Am I having an unhelpful thought right now?*

- *What would I say to a friend who was going through this situation and had this same thought?*

- *What might a calm version of me say about this?*

- *How might this look a few days from now?*

WHY IT WORKS

SEARCHING FOR FACTS HELPS YOU FIGURE OUT WHAT IS TRUE AND TURN DOWN YOUR ALARM SO YOU CAN THINK MORE CLEARLY, INSTEAD OF REACTING FROM UPSET FEELINGS.

When you use the P.A.U.S.E. strategy, there may be some time that goes by in between the steps of using a coping skill and searching for facts. That's because your thinking brain needs to come back online to be able to complete the last two steps of the P.A.U.S.E. strategy (searching for facts and encouraging yourself).

THOUGHTS, FEELINGS, AND FACTS

Now it's time to practice searching for facts. When we feel rejected, our brains sometimes tell us stories that *feel* true but might not actually be facts. Slowing down and separating thoughts, feelings, and facts can help us figure out which thoughts need a reality check.

For each scenario on the next two pages, ask yourself these questions:

- *What's the next thought that pops into my head?*
- *What's the feeling?*
- *What are the facts?*
- *What do I know that actually happened?*
- *What else could be true?*

 Skills for Rejection Sensitive Dysphoria

1. Your teacher didn't smile at you this morning, so she must be disappointed in you.

2. You sent a funny meme to your friend, but they read it 20 minutes ago and still haven't replied.

3. You offer an idea during a group discussion, and the other people briefly stop talking, and then the conversation continues without anyone mentioning your idea.

4. You get back a piece of writing with the teacher's notes written in red ink, asking you to fix two paragraphs so your work can be improved.

5. You see a photo on social media of your two closest friends hanging out without you.

6. You tried out a new basketball trick, and you immediately made a mistake in front of your whole gym class.

7. You are telling a story to a couple of friends, and one friend suddenly stops listening, checks their phone, and starts tapping impatiently.

8. You see your friend get a higher grade than you did.

9. You and a friend have a regular plan to eat lunch together. Today, your friend walks past you and sits down with someone else without saying anything.

10. You spent hours cleaning your room, but your parent walks in, points out one small item left on the floor, and says you're messy.

11. You share your artwork and someone next to you says, "That's kind of weird."

In the box below, draw or write about what surprised you and what you learned by searching for facts with each of the scenarios.

REFLECTION

STEPPING BACK FROM YOUR THOUGHTS

Thought distancing is a way to create a little space between you and your thoughts so they don't take over. Instead of getting pulled into the story, you learn to step back and notice the thought as something your brain is saying, not something you *have* to believe.

One simple way to practice thought distancing is by changing how you talk about your thoughts. Instead of saying "They don't like me," you can say **"I'm having the thought that they don't like me."** This small change reminds your brain that this is a thought and not a fact. You can also try phrases like **"I'm noticing my brain is telling me…"** or **"A thought is showing up that says…"** These phrases help calm your alarm and give your thinking brain more control.

WHY IT WORKS

THOUGHT DISTANCING WORKS BECAUSE IT HELPS YOU SEE THOUGHTS AS MENTAL MESSAGES, NOT AS FACTS THAT YOU HAVE TO BELIEVE.

We learned about the strategies for the letters P, A, U, and S. Now let's look at the strategy that goes along with the letter E.

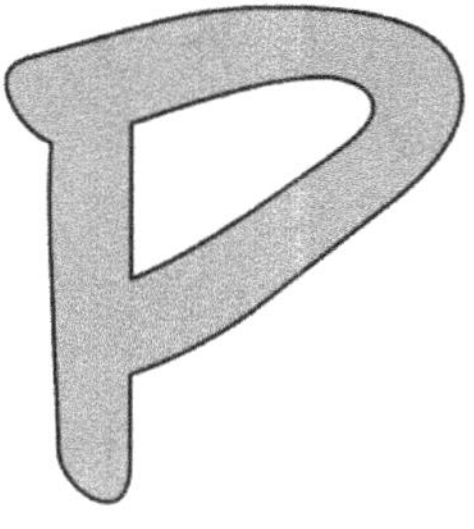

P AUSE, NOTICE YOUR ALARM, AND BREATHE

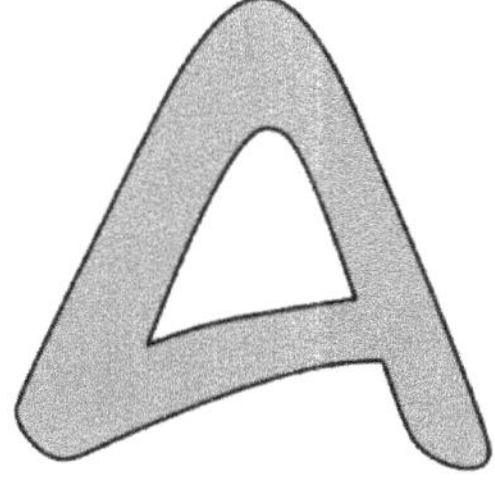

A LLOW AND NAME YOUR FEELINGS

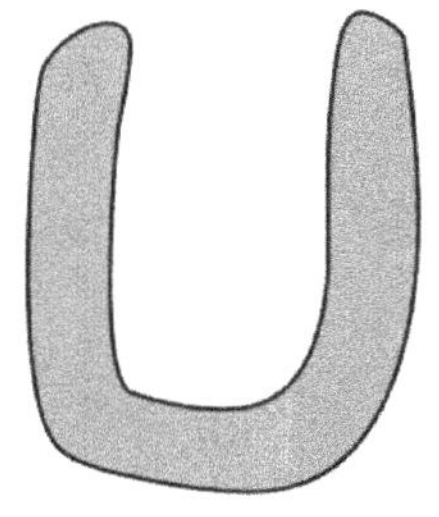

U SE A COPING SKILL

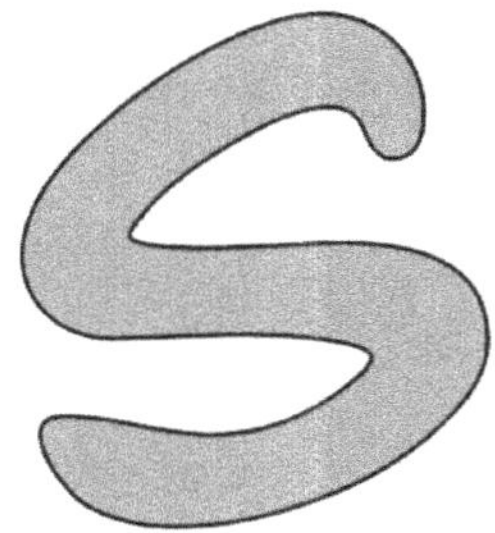

S EARCH FOR FACTS

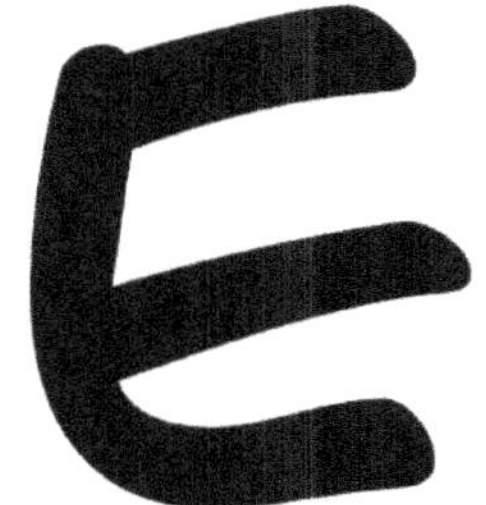

E NCOURAGE YOURSELF

YOUR INNER ENCOURAGER

The last step in the P.A.U.S.E. strategy stands for **Encourage Yourself**. This is where self-compassion comes in. When your rejection alarm goes off, the voice in your head can sound really mean. It might say things like "Everyone's mad at me," "I messed everything up," or "I'm not good enough." These thoughts are part of your inner alarm trying to protect you, but they usually make your feelings stronger and harder to manage.

Encouraging yourself means responding to those moments with helpful thoughts and compassion instead of criticism. Self-compassion doesn't mean pretending things don't hurt or telling yourself everything is fine. It means noticing that something is hard and choosing to support yourself through it anyway.

Your inner Encourager is the part of you that does exactly this. It's the opposite of your alarm. Your Encourager helps you remember that you're safe, capable, and worthy of belonging, even when things don't go perfectly. Your Encourager stands up to your alarm and offers a kinder, more realistic perspective.

Your Encourager doesn't ignore mistakes or feelings. Instead, it helps you find helpful thoughts that calm your alarm and helps you respond in ways that support you instead of hurting you.

In the box below, design your Encourager as a character using lines, colors, shapes, or symbols. You can make it serious, funny, strong, gentle, or creative. Add speech bubbles to write some of the helpful words your Encourager says. There's no right or wrong way to do this, just create a character that feels supportive to you.

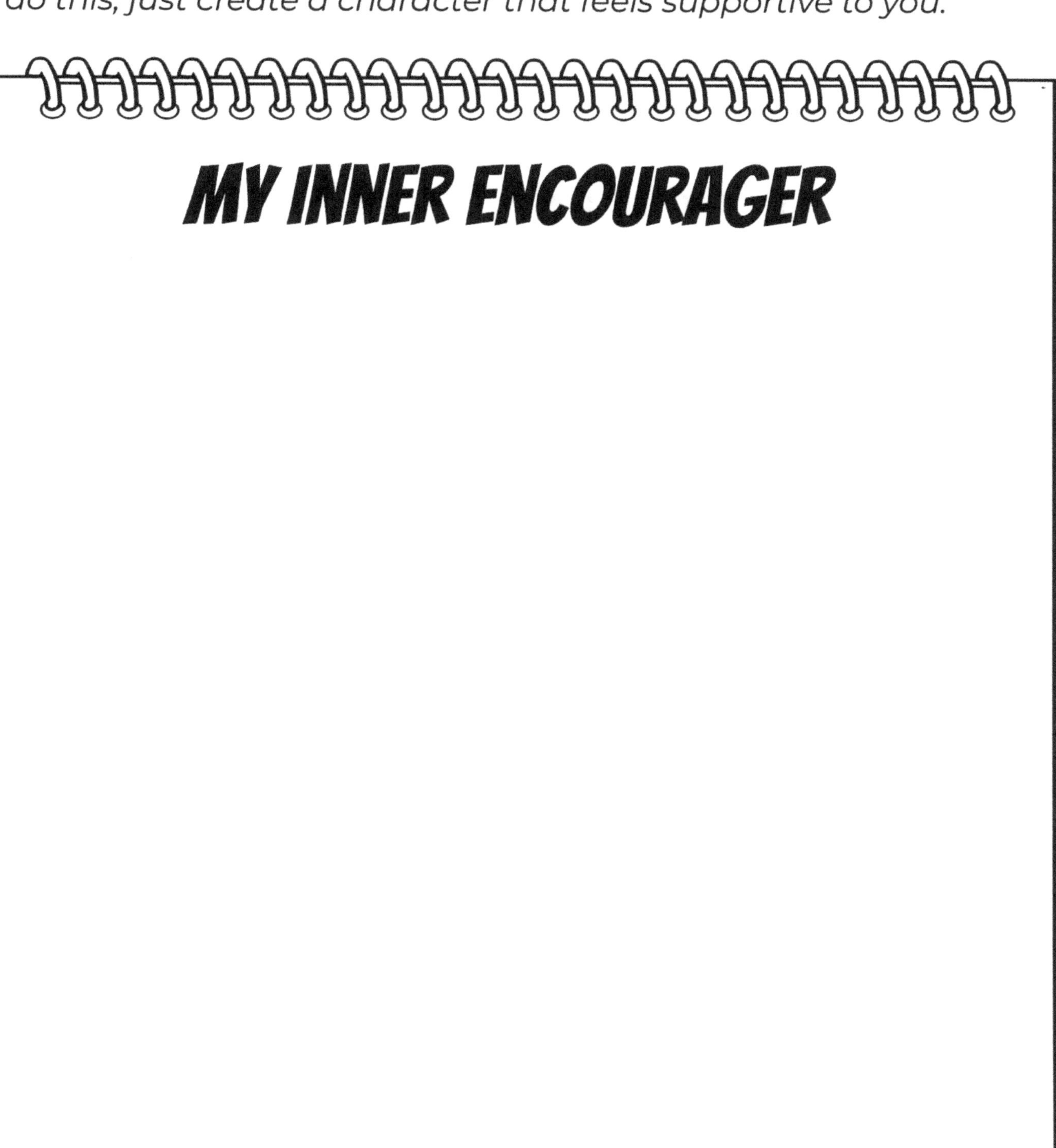
MY INNER ENCOURAGER

INTRODUCING...

Giving your Encourager a name reminds you that this calm, supportive voice is part of you, and you can choose to listen to it. Over time, the more you practice using and listening to your Encourager, the easier it'll become to find self-compassion and helpful thoughts when you need them.

MY ENCOURAGER'S NAME IS:

____

Write a note from your Encourager to yourself with words that would be helpful to hear during a challenging moment.

HELPFUL THOUGHTS TO TALK BACK

In the bubbles below, write some more realistic, kind, and self-compassionate words your Encourager might say to help quiet your alarm and support you.

SUPPORTIVE PEOPLE

When things feel hard, it can also be helpful to remember that you aren't doing life all on your own. Everyone has people who support them, care about them, and want them to do well. These might be family members, teachers, counselors, coaches, friends, or other trusted people who help you.

In the box below, write or draw the people who support you at home, at school, or in activities outside of school. When you think about these people, notice how your body feels. The feelings you notice are the same feelings your Encourager is helping you create inside yourself. You can imagine what helpful words your supportive people might say to you and let your Encourager borrow some of those same words.

THOUGHTS, FEELINGS, AND ACTIONS

Your Encourager's job is to speak to you with self-compassion and to help you manage your thoughts. Even though you can't see your thoughts, they still have a big impact on how you feel and how you act.

Your thoughts, feelings, and behavior are all connected. Your thoughts affect your feelings, and those feelings influence the choices you make, or your behavior. Your behavior then reinforces your thoughts, which creates a cycle. The good news is that when you learn to notice and change your thoughts, you can change how you feel. And when your feelings change, your behavior often changes too.

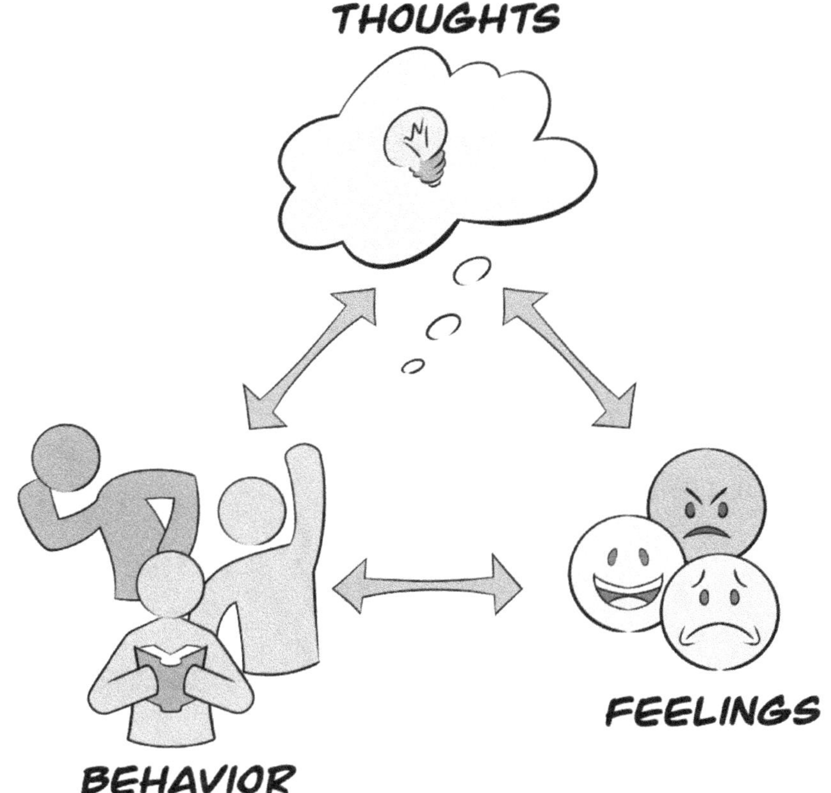

NOT EVERY THOUGHT DESERVES YOUR ATTENTION

As we learned, **not all thoughts are true or helpful**, especially when our inner alarms are loud. This is why we can't believe everything we think, and why we need to ask ourselves questions to search for the facts.

The thoughts that help us feel comfortable are called helpful thoughts. The thoughts that make us feel uncomfortable and make our feelings stronger and harder to manage are called unhelpful thoughts.

Unhelpful thoughts often sound extreme or harsh, like "This always happens" or "I'm not good enough," and they can make your body feel stressed or tense. Helpful thoughts don't pretend everything is perfect, but they do help you cope and keep things in perspective. When you practice swapping unhelpful thoughts for more helpful and realistic thoughts, you'll give your-self more control over your feelings instead of letting your alarm take over.

FLIPPING THOUGHTS

Practice flipping these unhelpful thoughts to make them more helpful and realistic.

You say hi to someone you know in the hallway, and they don't respond or seem to hear you. You think, "They're ignoring me. They don't like me." What helpful thought can you choose instead?

____

____

A coach gives you feedback after practice and doesn't say anything positive afterward. You think, "I must be bad. I should just quit the team." What helpful thought can you choose instead?

____

____

You raise your hand in class, but the teacher calls on someone else. You think, "My answer isn't good enough." What helpful thought can you choose instead?

____

____

You tell a joke and no one laughs. You think, "Everyone thinks I'm awkward." What helpful thought can you choose instead?

____

____

You walk into a room, and the conversation suddenly gets quiet. You think, "I'm not supposed to be here." What helpful thought can you choose instead?

____

____

Your parent sounds impatient and distracted when you ask them a question. You think, "They're annoyed with me." What helpful thought can you choose instead?

____

____

You notice a friend whispering to someone while glancing in your direction. You think, "They don't like me and they're talking badly about me." What helpful thought can you choose instead?

____

____

You answer a question and someone else corrects you. You think, "I'm embarrassed. I shouldn't have said anything." What helpful thought can you choose instead?

____

____

You are left out of being chosen first for something, even though you usually are. You think, "I don't matter as much anymore." What helpful thought can you choose instead?

____

____

A teacher uses your work as an example of what needs improvement. You think, "Everyone thinks I did a terrible job." What helpful thought can you choose instead?

____

____

You're invited out, but you learn that other people were invited earlier than you were. You think, "They don't even really like me." What helpful thought can you choose instead?

____

SELF-COMPASSION

Self-compassion means talking to yourself with the same kindness and understanding that you would give to a friend when they're hurting. It doesn't mean pretending that something didn't hurt or telling yourself everything is fine when it's not. It means noticing your pain while supporting yourself through it, instead of piling on shame.

When RSD hits, the brain often jumps to unhelpful thoughts that can make the pain feel bigger and last longer. Self-compassion helps by reminding your brain that you're safe, that this feeling makes sense, and that you're allowed to have strong emotions. When you treat yourself more gently, you can bounce back a little quicker.

As we learned, the first step in P.A.U.S.E. involves noticing your alarm. This is because naming the experience helps you step out of self-judgment and notice what's happening instead. You can also remind yourself that you're not alone. Many others feel this same kind of hurt too. You can choose a helpful thought like "I can handle this feeling" or "Even though this hurts, I'm still okay" or "I don't have to be perfect to belong." The goal of encouraging yourself with self-compassion isn't to make the feeling disappear, but to support yourself while it moves through you.

We need to talk after class.
Naming your feelings and experience helps you notice what's happening and step out of self-judgment.
Nothing's wrong with me. I'm not alone in feeling this way. Lots of other people have RSD too.
The goal is not to make your feelings disappear, but to support yourself as your feelings move through you.
Remind yourself that you're not alone. Many others feel this same kind of hurt, and having this reaction doesn't mean there's anything wrong with you.
I can handle this feeling.
Even though this hurts, I'm still okay.
I don't have to be perfect.
Choose a helpful thought.

AFTER THE ALARM

Sometimes your alarm will go off, and you'll react without using your tools. You might cry, snap, shut down, say something you didn't mean, and feel embarrassed afterward. This happens to a lot of people. If this happens to you it doesn't mean you've failed, you're bad, or the tools aren't working. It just means that your alarm took over in that situation because you're a human who's still growing and learning.

After a reaction, it's common for shame to show up in unhelpful thoughts like "Why did I do that?" or "I ruined everything" or "Everyone thinks I'm too much." These unhelpful thoughts can make you feel even worse. If you feel shame after a reaction, it can be hard to know what to do. You might want to disappear, over-explain, or say nothing at all. This is when repair may be useful, and we'll talk more about that on the next page.

The good news is, you can still use the P.A.U.S.E. strategy *after* a big reaction. Remember to talk to yourself with self-compassion, the way your Encourager would. Remind yourself that you can take time to calm down, and you're allowed to make mistakes. You don't need to practice all of the skills perfectly. You can repair, reset, and try again. What matters is how you support yourself and others afterward.

REPAIRING WITH OTHERS

After a reaction, you might want to fix things with others. A repair doesn't always have to be a big, long conversation. Sometimes a few simple, honest words with the other person are enough. Try this 3-step repair strategy:

1. **Apologize:**   I'm sorry that I...
2. **Own it:**   I was overwhelmed and my feelings took over.
3. **Next steps**:   Can we reset?

Here are some examples of the 3-step repair strategy:

- I'm sorry that I shut down and stopped responding. I had a big reaction and didn't handle it well. I'm calmer now. What can I do to make it better?

- I'm sorry that I reacted so strongly. I was overwhelmed and my emotions took control. This is something that I'm still working on. Thanks for giving me a minute. Can we talk about it now?

- I'm sorry that I walked away so suddenly. I was overwhelmed and needed space to calm down. I'll check back with you later today.

- I'm sorry but I can't talk about this right now. My feelings are still *really* strong. I'll be ready to talk in about 15 minutes.

- I'm sorry that I didn't respond right away. I needed time to calm my body and thoughts. Can we talk after I take a short break?

WHEN I FEEL CALM

In the body outline below, use colors, lines, shapes, symbols, or words to show what your body feels like when you're thinking helpful thoughts and feeling calm, safe, and supported.

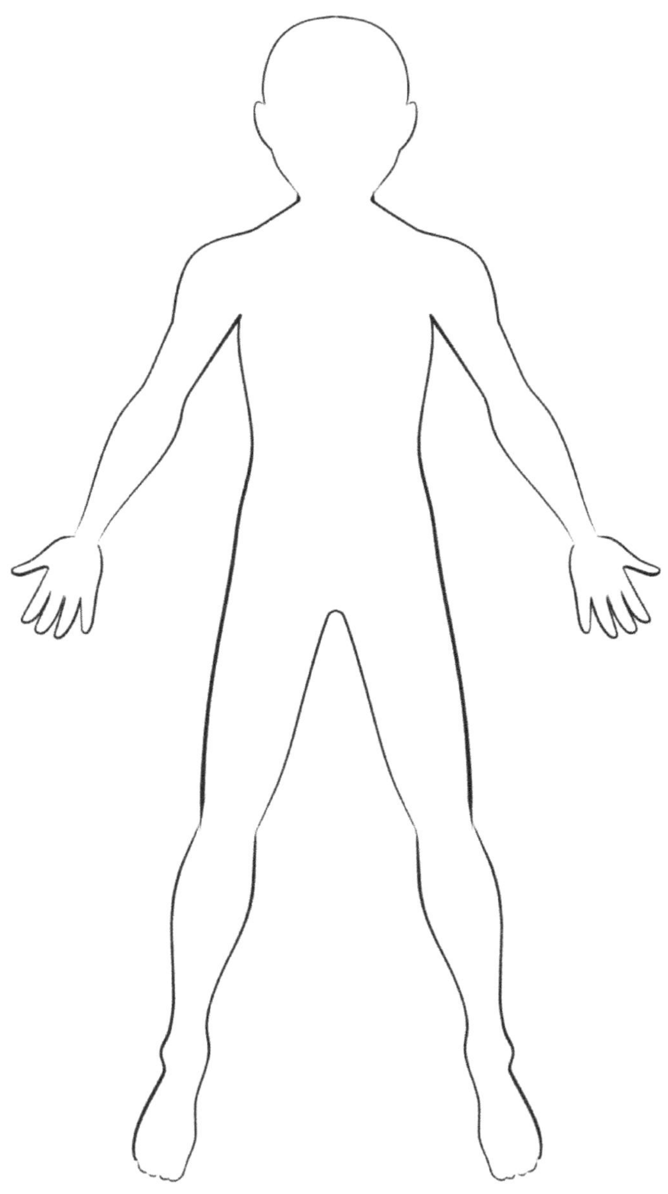

What do you notice when you compare this image with the first body map you made at the beginning of this workbook?

YOU HAVE CHOICES

Even after practicing the P.A.U.S.E. strategy a bunch of times, your rejection alarm will still go off sometimes. That doesn't mean you did anything wrong. It means your brain noticed something that felt like a threat to connection or belonging. Here's what can happen:

→ A trigger shows up.

→ Your alarm goes off.

→ Your body reacts.

→ Your thoughts get loud and harsh.

Before reading this book, this situation might have felt confusing and overwhelming. But now you understand what's happening inside you, so you have more choices and control.

Now when your alarm shows up, you can practice using your P.A.U.S.E. strategy. You can **P**ause, notice your alarm, and take a deep breath. Then **A**llow and name your feelings. Next, **U**se a coping skill. Then **S**earch for facts by asking yourself questions like "What proof do I have that it might not be true?" Last, **E**ncourage yourself with self-compassion and helpful thoughts like "I can handle this." You don't have to do each step perfectly, and you don't have to do every step each time. Even one small step will be useful! Every time you pause, breathe, or use even one coping skill, you're training your brain to handle these moments differently.

